Resurrection Rain

Resurrection Rain

Meditations for Holy Week

Arthur F. Fogartie

Geneva Press
Louisville, Kentucky

Book design by Sharon Adams
Cover design by Jennifer Cox

First edition

Published by Geneva Press
Louisville, Kentucky

This book is printed on acid-free paper that meets the American National Standards Institute Z39.48 standard. ∞

PRINTED IN THE UNITED STATES OF AMERICA

01 02 03 04 05 06 07 08 09 10 — 10 9 8 7 6 5 4 3 2 1

Library of Congress Cataloging-in-Publication Data

A catalog record for this book is available from the Library of Congress.

ISBN 0-664-50178-8

To the members of the
First Presbyterian Church of Warren, Arkansas,
. . . especially to those who are now in
Our Father's House:
"I thank my God in all my remembrance of you."

Contents

PALM SUNDAY

*

"Come into the Lord's presence with singing."

—Psalm 100:2

The Man Who Owned the Ass

e sat quietly, *listening to the wind* flowing with the faint rustle of some fine fabric over the low hills and into the hub of the miniature valley where his house stood. Easing down the slope, the breeze caressed the trees, tickled the tall grass, brushed his face with a dry kiss, then disappeared to wherever winds go to die.

He pushed back in his chair, ignoring the creaking protests of the canvas, until he had angled against the mud wall behind him. The sun sank behind the hills, slowly at first, then with increasing speed as it neared its celestial bed.

Color splashed the western horizon. He watched the yellow turn orange, then red, crimson, burgundy, violet, indigo, finally black.

The earth slept, guarded by a retinue of overseeing stars. And still he sat.

✳ ✳ ✳ ✳ ✳

The two men came early, walking into town almost simultaneously with the sun's first tentative peek over the horizon. Somehow, the minute I saw them, I knew they were coming here.

Strange men; poorly dressed, but clean. Powerfully built, short and wide. No sooner had they entered my gate than they went straight to work untying Yasheeth. I couldn't believe it. They were stealing my donkey right in front of my house!

I wasn't particularly worried about the thieves, though. The minute one of those ragamuffins put a saddle across her back, Yasheeth would kick in his teeth. And if they tried to lead her away, she'd just balk and sit down. Yasheeth doesn't like strangers, and she won't go anywhere without her morning apple. So, I peered out of the window and prepared to enjoy the show.

And what entertainment! The leads to Yasheeth's halter, soaked with the morning dew, had hardened into rocks, and the men swore and strained at the knots. Still, the thieves seemed pretty self-assured. They shouted, laughed, howled, and pushed one another. Stealth was hardly their strong point.

"Andrew," said the shorter of the two in mock horror, "I've been away from the nets too long. Look at my hand. A blister! I've turned delicate. I'll be mistaken for a pampered nobleman."

"Simon," the other replied, "with your face, you'll never be accused of nobility. Skin like leather. Come to think of it, you look a lot like someone's old boot. Hey! Watch it! You almost got sand in my eye!"

"Keep a respectful tongue in your head, or I'll throw some more, dear brother. Here, give me your knife. I don't want to muss my manicure with this hemp any longer."

The one called Andrew laughed. "You're in a foolish enough mood, Simon. That's it, one more cut. Okay, let's go."

Taking hold of the tattered leads, they walked off. They'd gone almost fifty steps before I realized they were not going to try to ride the colt. Neither had Yasheeth pitched her expected fit.

"Stop, thief!" I ran out the door. And they did. Stop, I mean. Standing halfway out of my gate, the men stared back at me with a mixture of confusion and amazement.

Very strange: thieves who joked their way through a crime and halted the minute you accosted them. No swords, no clubs, not even a menacing glare. Just two men gazing in genuine bewilderment at the frantic figure calling after them.

I'd been ready to summon down the wrath of Jehovah, but as I stood there, no more than fifteen feet away, I felt rather stupid. I had no sandals, no robe, only my short tunic. I hadn't even brushed my hair. I must have looked like a crazy man. The thieves barely restrained their giggles.

"Where are you taking Yasheeth?"

"Who? Oh, the little colt, fine young animal. Are you the owner? You must be proud to have such a marvelously gentle beast."

"She's not gentle at all," I snapped. "She's kicked me more times than I can remember. And stubborn? Oh, she'll never go anywhere I want. She's most uncooperative."

Insanity! Standing in the middle of the street discussing my colt's demeanor with the men who were, at that very moment, stealing her.

Simon sniggered, "Perhaps, my friend, you lack our experience with animals."

Both men dissolved in laughter.

"Never mind! Why are you stealing my donkey?"

"There's an ugly word, Andrew—'stealing.' You said this had all been arranged." Then to me, "No, sir, we're not pilfering. We're borrowing your little animal. The Master has need of her. We'll return her later today."

"I don't care if King Herod wants her. You can't just walk in here and wander off with my colt. She's never been ridden. She's never pulled a cart. As a matter of fact, she's scheduled for consecration during Passover."

Andrew moved closer, as if afraid someone would overhear. "She will be consecrated today. The Master has need of her. Please."

So, they left me standing there, speechless. I thought about chasing them until I heard a high-pitched laugh. Turning around, I saw little Ruth, the next-door neighbor's girl. For a minute I didn't understand. Then, she pointed, and I realized I didn't have anything on but my underwear.

I stomped back inside. "What's the world coming to? Strangers stealing donkeys and children without any manners."

* * * * *

An hour or so later, I headed outside again. Of course, I ran right into little Ruth, who turned and whispered to her mother. Though the woman tried hard not to look at me, I know I blushed.

I'd never seen a larger crowd. Every year we greet the Passover pilgrims traveling to Jerusalem. Since our town's only a little way from the city gates, our citizens act as welcomers for the travelers.

The tradition has slipped some in the past few years. Folks just aren't as interested anymore, I guess. I have no great zeal for pilgrimages either, but I've always liked greeting the strangers.

Anyway, today the size of the crowd seemed more like the old days. Almost everyone from Bethany came out, and quite a few from Bethphage.

When he passed, everyone began to stir. Some hollered to be saved (from what I don't know). Others requested favors. A mother held out her crippled son. Some young men kept shouting questions.

He rode by, seated on Yasheeth, who seemed perfectly at home with a passenger. As he passed, the man seldom acknowledged the crowd. He might have nodded at me. I'm not sure, but the two thieves, Simon and Andrew, picked me out. One of them shouted, "I see you found your clothes!"

Then they were all gone. The crowd wandered off, but I stayed a while, transfixed by the traveler's sad eyes. Had he been crying? I watched until the procession disappeared toward Jerusalem.

A few others stayed, too. Some prayed, others simply stared. One little boy began to recite from the prophets:

Rejoice greatly, O daughter of Zion!
  Shout aloud, O daughter of Jerusalem!
Lo, your king comes to you;
  Triumphant and victorious is he,
Humble and riding on an ass,
  on a colt, the foal of an ass.

Then I turned and went home.

* * * * *

The earth slept, guarded by a retinue of over-seeing stars. And still he sat.

The wind stirred again, irritating the bells on Yasheeth's halter.

"I'm coming, little one," he said. "You've had a long day. I should have bedded you sooner."

Brushing the little animal, he couldn't help feeling he'd been a part of something important. The thieves, the crowd, the parade, and now the sad-eyed Galilean asleep inside: "Tomorrow I return to Jerusalem, and I know I've already troubled you by borrowing the colt, but could I find an empty corner of your house in which to stay the night?"

Strange, a man he'd never seen before today, now a guest in his home. He threw an extra measure of grain into Yasheeth's feed box. "Sleep well, little one. You've earned it."

By the time he arose in the morning, the stranger was gone, and except for a new garland of wildflowers Yasheeth wore, no evidence existed to prove his guest had ever been there.

Yet he felt good about everything that had happened. Had he said "no," what would the Galilean have ridden? Where would he have slept?

No one had ordered him. No one had promised anything. He had just responded to a simple summons:

The Master has need of it.

MONDAY

✳

"For what will it profit them if they gain the whole world but forfeit their life?"

—Matthew 16:26

Fred Fenster Meets Joshua

*O*f all the parts of the church service, Fred Fenster liked the sermon the most. Oh, he hardly got goosepimples from all the exhortation and encouragement—in fact, any presentation remotely approaching the emotional absolutely turned him off.

No, Fred liked to think of each sermon as an intellectual athletic contest—like a tennis match—Fred vs. the preacher for the day. He'd sharpened his critical approach to a razor's edge. It was a science, a talent, an art form.

The introduction approximated the serve, which should be bold and brash—verbal thunder, oratorical lightning. Take charge, seize the audience by the throat. To the aggressive belong the listeners.

Like a Grand Slam champion, the successful speaker ought to follow the serve with booming points of interest and drive them home with the crisp volleys of telling illustrations.

Admittedly, preachers had been known to score on Fred. On those rare occasions, Fred paused, mentally applauded the homiletical agility, complimented the speaker with a curt nod, and then, once again, set about the task of the cerebral evisceration of whatever remained of the sermon. But preachers' points came few and far between.

Years of experience had made Fred a grizzled veteran—the master of charging a weakly stroked sentence or a sloppily executed story. Anything that floated, anything weak, anything not properly pinpointed found itself annihilated by the thundering overhead smash of sermonic criticism.

The time for the appointed match had come.

Worshipers settled into their pews like spectators in the bleachers . . .

the choir attentively occupied their box seats . . .

the minister trudged up the stairs toward the center court of the pulpit . . .

and Fred, the umpire, the supreme arbiter of competence and inefficiency, settled into his customary pose . . .

tucked neatly into the outside corner of the pew . . .

body tilted slightly to accommodate the angle . . .

left leg over right . . .

right arm along the pew back . . . left languishing over the rail.

Fred scrutinized the preacher with a benevolent earnestness that belied his mental savagery while giving the unsuspecting speaker the false impression of having at least one totally captivated listener. On the outside, Fred appeared relaxed. Inside, however, his mind leaned forward expectantly on its toes as he prepared to lash at the morning message.

The minister—a guest—Fred always liked guests . . . new style . . . different approach . . . usually brought one of their "greatest hits" along—bowed in prayer and then began:

> *Our text this morning comes from the twenty-fourth chapter of Joshua, where we find the great warrior chieftain addressing his contemporaries and recalling for them the mighty acts of God in history.*

"Ohhhhh no!" A wave of disbelief submerged Fred. "That's his best stuff? Pathetic!"

An elbow in the side from his wife reminded Fred not to whisper to himself. He fell silent—dismayed and disappointed.

The sermon plowed on. The preacher turned the corner and headed for the first point.

> *Friends, Joshua struggled to remind the Israelites of the Lord's presence. And this morning, I want to remind all of you that **God still works in the world.***

Fred groaned. "'God still works in the world.' Good grief. I can get that trite pablum on the cable at home. 'Surrender to Jesus—He lives and he will help you.'"

It might have ended that way because Fred lost interest. Some time ago he'd abandoned "shooting cripples" on the grounds they offered no intellectual challenge—so when a particularly weak sermon reared its mangy and uninspired head, Fred usually took little mental trips elsewhere. And he was wandering off—to somewhere luxurious and lazy, far removed from the confines of the sanctuary—when something happened.

What caused it was never clear, but Fred's mind suddenly erupted in a series of bright flashes like photographic slides clicking on and off in his head. Some flipped by so rapidly he only sensed them. Others burned their way deep into his memory.

Somewhere in a great mental vortex, a voice whispered,

> *in the world . . . still works in the world . . .*

and the pictures snapped into focus . . .

> the retired couple who, despite increasing health costs, higher energy bills, and decreasing incomes, still made their generous annual gift to the United Way campaign in which Fred worked . . .

> the boss shooing everyone out the door at noon on Christmas Eve provided they all went by the Children's Hospital to sing a few carols before heading home . . .

> Al Smith—sorry, old, drunk Al Smith— showing up in a worn but clean suit— sob—looking for a job. When someone finally gave him a break, he'd done okay.

Nice things, but how much God actually had to do with them, Fred wasn't sure. He shook his

head and cleared it just long enough to tune in
the preacher for a moment:

> *Joshua stood before the nation and
> said, "If you are unwilling to serve the
> Lord, [then] choose this day whom you
> will serve, but as for me and my house,
> we will serve the Lord."*
>
> *You see, friends, the old warrior was
> willing to **profess** his faith. Are you?*

"What?" Fred bolted upright. "Who does he
think he is? Wanders into our church and asks if
we profess our faith. What does that idiot think
we do every week—recite Mother Goose? Profess
my faith, indeed."

✳ ✳ ✳ ✳ ✳

Had the family been outside, Fred would have
assumed they were huddling together to keep
warm. But the two big folks with their accompanying brood of five little ones stood indoors,
bunched to one side of the bustling airport breeze-
way. They were not cold. They were praying.

Talbert laughed when he saw them. "Hey, Fred!
Get a load of the Jesus freaks over there."

Fred's initial reaction was to tell Talbert to
"Shut up." Given the recent spate of air disasters
and near misses, not to mention almost daily
reports of shoddy aircraft maintenance, Fred
didn't much feel like getting on a flight un-prayed
for, either. Besides, what he sensed for the family
was not ridicule but respect.

As he turned to silence his sneering companion, Fred remembered who Talbert was—the single, largest customer serviced by Fred's company. If Talbert took his business elsewhere, it could be a long, cold winter at the Fenster house. Discretion being valor's better half, Fred held his tongue.

✳ ✳ ✳ ✳ ✳

Once again the sermon snipped at him:

> "... *but as for me and my household, we will serve the Lord.*"

> *You see, brothers and sisters in Christ, Joshua was willing to **share** his faith.*

No lag ... no protest ... only the crystalline mental image of Eddie Hammett. Eddie just came to town—joined the company about four months ago. Nice guy, Eddie—lovely wife ... three attractive kids ... a well-behaved Cocker Spaniel.

Eddie inherited a pretty good amount from his folks. Oh, he worked very hard—Fred respected that. Eddie's good fortune just meant he had some very nice things—one of which was a first-rate lake house.

"Why don't you bring everybody out to the lake next Sunday, Fred?" Eddie's voice was always cheerful and genuine. "We'll swim and ski a little—burn a little red meat on the grill and make a day of it."

Fred had a better idea. The Hammetts were new—they surely didn't have a church yet. Fred started to say, "Eddie, that's great, but could we change the plan a little? The kids are supposed to sing in the year-end musical during church this Sunday. Tell you what—you come with us to worship. We'll have everything ready, change at the church, and head out. Stays light until about nine, so we'll have lots of time."

But a little voice inside started to mumble something about mixing business and religion, or being holier-than-thou, or looking like a sap or something like that. So Fred shook Eddie's hand and said, "Tell you what, Eddie. We've already got some plans—nothing real big, but something we can't get out of—you know how that is. Can we make it another time?"

* * * * *

That dad-gum preacher kept breaking in:

> " . . . *if you are unwilling to serve the Lord, choose this day whom you will serve . . . "*

> *Finally, friends, Joshua was willing to **live** his faith.*

"Live the faith . . . live the faith . . . live the faith." The words ping-ponged around inside Fred's head growing more intense with every ricochet. "Live the faith . . . live the faith."

The joke wasn't funny. Fred hadn't ever cared very much either for racial humor or for the guy who always seemed to have at least one new scurrilous story every time they played golf.

Fred could have left the room—no one would have stopped him. On a less theatrical note, he could have simply refrained from laughing. Crude, ethnically oriented jokes struck him as items more degrading to those telling and hearing them than to their intended targets. But for the sake of "the boys"—the old "male bonding" thing—he guffawed right along with the rest, some of whom nearly fell over.

His mind rolodexed to another image—his nineteen-year-old daughter gaping at him.

"You bought *that* stock? Daddy, I don't believe it! Don't you remember the report I put together for poli sci? I told you all about it a few weeks ago.

"That company makes most of its money from overseas operations in underdeveloped countries. With the help of crooked officials, it builds huge factories on land it purchases from uninformed and uneducated locals. The company pays barebones prices and makes glittering promises it never keeps. Then it hires the former landowners to work and pays them substandard wages for hours and hours of grueling and dangerous work.

"No child labor laws ... no environmental restrictions ... slipshod safety standards. So, they destroy local society while they beat the land to death. You've always prided yourself on the fact that your company sets very high standards. You cannot possibly support activity like that."

Well, he *had* invested. After all, with his business acumen, he knew a good deal when he saw one. Yes, Fred fully realized what was going on before he made the purchase. Who in the world can ignore the passionate ravings of an irate, socially conscious college student?

Still, the investment looked hot and the last few financial moves had not quite panned out as he had hoped. But this one was perfect. What a sweet score—the stock soared and Fred made some significant money.

But his daughter would not even try on the new outfit he bought her from some of the proceeds.

Didn't make any sense. How could he pass up a pure windfall? His refusal to invest was not going to bring about the collapse of that company. No, if he passed over the golden egg, someone else would snatch it up for sure.

✳ ✳ ✳ ✳ ✳

"What did you say, dear?" Fred spoke to his wife unsure exactly how they'd gotten into the center aisle. And how in the world had he missed the final hymn and benediction? They shuffled toward the door and he asked again, "What did you say?"

"I said, 'He wasn't the greatest preacher I ever heard, but wasn't the conclusion excellent?'"

"I guess. What was it?"

"Honestly, Fred! You have got to think less about tennis and more about theology—at least in church. He said, *'Today you and I must make a choice—we have to choose like Joshua—we have to choose in front of our friends and families, our coworkers and our neighbors'*—something like that.

"But I remember his last sentence exactly. He said, *'Make your choice, because there's nothing in this world more miserable than a half-hearted Christian.'* Isn't that terrific?"

"Yeah, terrific."

Outside the church, the sun smiled on a perfect autumn day . . .

the air smelled distinctly of fall . . .

birds chirped and squirrels chattered . . .

every stepped-on, fallen leaf crackled with Joshua's voice:

Choose this day whom you will serve . . .

And Fred Fenster walked toward his house a very troubled man.

TUESDAY

"If any of you suffers as a Christian, do not consider it a disgrace."

—Matthew 4:16

The Man Who
Lived Up to His Name

he old man sat next to the window, his feet on a stool, a thick blanket protecting his legs from the chill. Staring out at his frolicking grandchildren, he smiled as he remembered the days he raced the wind across the hills outside Colossae.

But his carefree hours of youth had ended abruptly on the day of his father's death. Funny how quickly the child transforms into an adult when the situation demands it. And Philemon's metamorphosis had not taken very long. One minute, a youngster concerned only with the starting time of the next game, and the next, a merchant, driven by creditors and responsibilities.

Oh, he'd made it. Made it? He'd positively flourished. But that had been so long ago.

So many days gone. So many friends departed. So much water under so many bridges. And yet, somehow the scroll and what it represented made everything else dwindle into insignificance.

It lay on his lap, nestled among the folds of the blanket. A small scroll, hardly worth noticing, actually, but Philemon counted it his prized possession. Once again he picked it up, loosed the twine, smoothed it across his thighs, and read the salutation:

> *Paul, a prisoner of Christ Jesus, and Timothy our brother, to Philemon our dear friend and co-worker, to Apphia our sister, to Archippus our fellow soldier, and to the church in your house: Grace to you and peace from God our Father and the Lord Jesus Christ.*

How many letters Paul had written to the Colossian church Philemon couldn't even remember. But he'd kept this one—this one had been addressed especially to him. While he absent-mindedly adjusted the comforter over the once-strong thighs that would never race again, Philemon thought back.

✷ ✷ ✷ ✷ ✷

On the day the letter came, the sun shone with a vengeance, baking the air to lung-searing intensity. As if afraid to attract the heat's animosity, nothing moved. Even the insects postponed their daily assault on the herd.

Little Adrian was studying his lessons in the scrawny shade of a palm tree. Suddenly, he shouted toward the house, "Mother, Father, a caravan! A caravan! Someone's coming. Quick, come and see!"

Sure enough, a small procession inched its way toward the estate. The shimmering of the roasted air made the meager band appear to stagger along its route.

Apphia, unruffled and characteristically effi-
cient, coolly directed the servants and set them to
preparing refreshments, drawing baths, and
readying the guest quarters. The laws of hospi-
tality demanded nothing less than an open-armed
reception regardless of the travelers' identities.

A little later, while still some way off, the caravan paused. A man, a young man, skidded from
the back of a donkey, waved his thanks, and
trudged toward the house. To Philemon's surprise, Apphia's dismay, and the servants' disgust,
the desert train continued on its way. All the
preparations were for nothing. No one even
requested a cup of water. They just left!

But the youthful, erstwhile traveler doggedly
approached the house. The nearer he drew, the
more familiar he seemed: tall, slender, well-
muscled, with jet-black hair. Then, recognition,
and with it a flood of conflicting emotions . . . joy
and anger . . . pleasure and resentment . . . the
urge to shout, the urge to snarl.

Adrian identified the traveler, too. All at once
oblivious to the heat, the youngster rushed across
the lawn clapping his hands, and coiled himself
around the visitor's leg. "Onesimus, Onesimus! I
thought you'd never come back."

With a broad smile canyoning his face, the
vagabond patted Adrian on the head. "Later, little
one. We'll have time to play later. First, I must
speak to your father."

The grin vanished as Onesimus stood before
Adrian's father. "Master Philemon, I have
returned. Running away was a bad thing, I know.

I realize you have the right to punish me. I will accept whatever penalty you see fit to dispense. But before you pronounce judgment, I humbly request a few moments. We have some things to discuss."

Philemon opened his mouth to speak, then stopped. Onesimus had used his staff to scratch out an arch in the dirt. Far from the random doodling of a nervous man, the stroke had been deliberate.

Philemon slowly descended the porch stairs. With his eyes locked on the runaway, the richest man in Colossae made another arch in the dust with his toe, one that started at the point of the first and bisected it. The crisscrossed lines formed the crude outline of a fish—the symbol known only to the followers of The Way.

Unable to hide his surprise, Philemon gawked at the young man. "Yes, Onesimus. It appears we do, indeed, have a good many things to go over."

On their way into the house, Onesimus handed Philemon a small scroll.

✳ ✳ ✳ ✳ ✳

Philemon read the letter, then looked up. "So, you know my friend Paul?"

"Yes. A mutual friend introduced us in Ephesus. Paul instructed me in The Way. It took a while because I had a lot to learn, and some of what Paul said sounded so strange. But now I, too, am a Christian!"

"A what?"

"A Christian. Oh, you probably haven't heard the term. It's pretty new. Most say it started in Antioch. Hecklers used it as an insult, but now we wear the label with pride. Christians, you know, the people of The Way, followers of the Christ."

"I see." Philemon stared at the far wall as if searching for what to say. "Onesimus, Paul asks me to take you back, to restore you to the household, to forgive. I am not unswayed by his argument. He is, as you know firsthand, a very wise and judicious man, and a trusted friend. But I must hear from you. I need to understand why you ran away."

"Master Philemon, my flight troubled you, and still does, I can see. I'm not sure where to begin except to say you contributed nothing to my leaving. I never felt abused or mistreated. As much as I can be, I am a member of this household. Little Adrian treats me like his older brother.

"But it never seemed—uh, I never felt free. You never denied me anything. I could come and go. I traveled with you and with Lady Apphia, but I was not on my own. The longer I considered what lay beyond this house, this family, my duties, the more compelling it became. I had to see. I had to roam free to do as I pleased when I pleased.

"When I got away, when I reached Ephesus, I didn't feel right. Oh, I had fun—did lots of things I'd never done. I kept my own house, slept when I wished, and went where I wanted. But, after a few weeks, I realized I still wasn't free. License and freedom are not the same. Snatched freedom granted me no real liberty.

"Paul told me something very strange, but very intriguing. 'Onesimus,' he said, 'the Lord Christ sets us free not only to sin but also not to sin.' It took me a while to figure out what he meant.

"When we're told not to do something, the forbidden things loom with allure and enticing attractiveness. But once we're told we can have or do whatever we want, we eventually see how shallow and meaningless the forbidden was. The Master tells us, 'Go, and do as you please. But whatever you do, remember I love you and you love me. All your life, your deeds reflect how you feel about me.'

"Once I understood that my freedom in Christ turned me loose to do as I please, I realized what I really want to do is serve him. When Paul and I discussed my decision, he pointed out that I could not fulfill my desire with the cloud of my sin against you hanging over me.

"Master Philemon, I ask your forgiveness and restoration."

Silence rumbled across the room. Finally, Philemon spoke. "Well said, Onesimus. And yet Paul understands full well what I can do to you. The law stands firmly on my side. Without consulting anyone, I can have you flogged, branded, imprisoned, or even executed. It is my right. Why did he send you back?"

A plaintive smile danced across Onesimus's lips. "Freedom, Master Philemon. Paul understands you are free to do with me what you wish. Set free by the laws of Rome to punish. Set free by the Law of Love to forgive. Both Paul and I know you are a Christian. For us, that is enough."

✳ ✳ ✳ ✳ ✳

So long ago . . . so fresh in his memory.

Philemon reached across the table and yanked the bell cord. Almost immediately, a servant entered.

"Yes, sir?"

"Gideon, I want you to take something to Ephesus."

"Certainly, sir. What do you wish for me to carry?"

"This." Philemon carefully rerolled the scroll, bound it, and slipped it into its own special silk cover. "Take this to a man named Onesimus. Tell him . . . tell him, 'Master Philemon says, I'm glad you lived up.'"

"Pardon me?"

"He will understand. Now go."

Philemon stretched to ease the stiffness creeping across his shoulders and gazed, once more, across the yard. How times change—the swiftest of the swift now an old man living out his dotage. Apphia, gone lo these many years. Adrian, a father and the successful heir to the family enterprise. And the former runaway, now Onesimus, bishop of the church at Ephesus.

Philemon grinned, "Onesimus turned out to be a very accurate name. Paul understood that when he wrote to me. 'Useful.' Onesimus means 'useful.' What Paul said was true," he pointed out:

> *Formerly he was useless to you, but now he is indeed useful.*

Once Philemon's slave had been "Onesimus" in name only. Now, he was "Onesimus" in nature as well.

The old man thought again of the other name, the one introduced by Onesimus on the day of his return: "Christian"—a follower of the Christ.

Philemon eased back into his chair in preparation for his afternoon nap. "Christian. Christian. What a grand name. I wonder how many will be able to live up to it?"

WEDNESDAY

*

"This is my commandment, that you love one another."

—John 15:12

On Closer Inspection

w, nuts!"

Another paper wad arched across the room, banked off the wall, and plopped into the trash can.

"Well, at least I haven't lost my touch."

I looked over at the wastebasket. Close to two dozen little crumpled-paper basketballs lay around the can's base. I was vastly overestimating my shooting. Another myth destroyed.

The tablet on my desk glared at me, and for what seemed the hundredth time, I scribbled the words of my text across the top of the page.

It had started off like any other Friday. Sermon day. Everything appeared ready: the notes, historical data, musings, illustrations—all there. Now to mold everything into a coherent presentation.

For a while, the process cruised along. Just another Friday. Just another sermon. At least, until Henry showed up.

Henry serves the church across the street. Every Friday morning he comes over for a visit. Our little confabs have assumed a ritualistic flavor.

After drumming his distinctive tattoo on my outside door, Henry sticks his head in: "Is His Eminence receiving today?"

My reply never varies: "Only high ranking officials of the Kingdom," and the session begins. We consume considerable coffee, and banter back and forth. Then, at a time known only to him, Henry invariably asks: "What's the message this week, Doctor?"

Since I've been in town longer than Henry, and therefore represent the senior member of our two-man ecclesiastical society, Henry has awarded me an honorary doctorate. For a while I ignobly suspected Henry wanted to discuss my sermon in hopes of finding help for his sermon. We have been known to attempt the same text in the same week. But after a while I realized Henry's interest springs purely from academic curiosity.

Before entering the pastorate, he'd been a teacher, and I think he misses the intellectual duels into which he'd fall with his colleagues. Besides, if he wanted to steal, he could find better sources.

Henry had arrived right on time. Over coffee and a few too many doughnuts, we traded opinions on current events, particularly the baseball divisional standings and all-star voting. Finally, with a knowing grin and great production, Henry asked, "Tell me, Doctor, what is the message for the week?"

"A little different this week, my friend," I began. "We're not going anywhere. We've gotten sluggish. Oh, attendance holds up okay, but our financial picture stinks! The choir does all right, but I bet they haven't recruited a new voice in two years. And the church suppers, boy, oh boy, same old people, same old food, same old programs.

"We're taking two steps backward for each one we take forward. No progress—no drive! We're settling into the summer slump. It's time to light a fire under these people."

Henry chuckled, "Do you have a text, or are you just gonna flap your arms and yell?"

"A great text, Henry. A classic! Bet you've preached it fifteen times. Joshua's rallying cry:

> Now if you are unwilling to serve the Lord, choose this day whom you will serve . . . but as for me and my household, we will serve the Lord.

Henry thought a minute. "That's a good one, all right. How are you gonna play it?"

"Head on, Henry. Full bore. I've tried subtle stuff with no effect, so I'm taking off the kid gloves. As I see it, we're faced with a matter of priorities. We have to get our ducks in a row. Decide what's important. You know, 'choose this day.'

"First, I'm talking about time. We've got folks who never see the inside of the building except on an occasional Sunday morning. Why they come then I don't know. Habit, guilt, appearances, it's beyond me. It's sad, Henry. Some of my people could do great things for the church, but they'd rather pay homage to the great god of convenience."

Henry just sat, quietly.

"Then, I'm starting in on money. Stewardship season starts in October, but I want to get the ball rolling a little early. My people don't give what they should. We have more country club memberships, foreign cars, beach houses, and European trips than all the other churches combined!

"Still, people don't give. They have a thousand excuses. Truth is, though, they just don't want to let loose of the bucks. We operate on a shoestring. Ridiculous! I tell you. Sunday, I'm turning some pockets inside out!"

Henry shifted in his chair.

"Then, behavior! We've got some real sharks. Sam Bennett would slit his own mother's throat for a dollar. Old Lady Elliot's the biggest gossip in town, maybe in the entire state. She'll say anything about anybody, yours truly included. Well, I'm taking care of that!"

The sermon now resembled a stampeding herd of cattle. I honestly hadn't intended to take quite such a hard line, but the more I waxed eloquent, the better I sounded. I carried on for a while longer, and by the time I finished, you could singe paper on my forehead. I fairly frothed with inspiration. I wanted to preach now!

"Henry, old buddy, we've made this too easy. Want to join, fine. Don't want to come, fine. Won't contribute, fine. Well, Sunday ends the

picnic. We're going to change a few things around
here.

"I'll lay 'em out. I can just see the ones who will
squirm. They'll be dying to escape. Don't let your
flock out early, they'll get trampled in the rush."

Henry seemed far less enthused by my impend-
ing oration than I had hoped. Usually, he perched
on the front of his chair, hanging on every word.
Today, though, he slouched in his seat, lips
pursed, a vacant look in his eye.

When I paused to take a breath, Henry stood
and shook my hand. "Thank you, Doctor. See you
next week."

Before I could protest, he'd closed the door
behind him. I wondered about his atypical behavior momentarily, but I had things to do. I straight-
ened my papers and went back to work.

❊ ❊ ❊ ❊ ❊

So, there I sat. Nothing happened. As if log-
jammed in the pen, the words would not flow. I
pounded on the sermon for the next hour, but I
couldn't stop thinking about Henry. His usual
effervescence and quick wit routinely pulled us
into a theological Ping-Pong match. He'd nitpick
and congratulate, laugh at the humorous and
reject the trite. But not today. He'd just gone
home.

To clear my head, I took a stroll around the
church. Down the hall, through the classrooms,
an occasional chord plucked on an occasional
piano, past the fellowship hall, a word of greeting

to the Meals on Wheels staff and a piece of cake for my efforts, and finally, as usual, into the sanctuary.

I scrutinized the pulpit from the back row, trying to visualize the sermon. What seemed so crystal clear only an hour before had taken on the consistency of mental oatmeal. Great impenetrable clouds settled between my ears and I couldn't quite remember what I'd said.

Something was wrong. The pulpit looked funny, out of kilter, lopsided. What was it?

The Bible. I always keep the big pulpit Bible opened to the Twenty-third Psalm because it's pretty close to the middle and everything looks nice and symmetrical. But now, there were too many pages on the right side, as I looked at it. Some kids had messed with it again.

Hoisting myself out of the pew, I trudged down the aisle mumbling vague threats, climbed the pulpit steps, and reached to return the Bible to its authorized position. Then I noticed the sheet of paper lying lengthwise across the page. I read the passage the paper underlined:

> *You hypocrite, first take the log out of your own eye, and then you can see clearly to take the speck out of your brother's eye.*

The words began to pulsate, larger and larger:

> *You hypocrite!*

The longer I considered my comment regarding time, the more transparent it became. Sure, I passed a lot of hours at the church, but my study's there. I come down in the evenings several times a week, but almost exclusively when I'm involved in some official capacity, and often accompanied by a good deal of complaining. It dawned on me I'd long since quit going to church; I went to work!

You hypocrite!

I remembered the bull sessions when I sat with friends and raked other people over the verbal coals, laughing at their idiosyncrasies, criticizing their efforts, questioning their capabilities, and assassinating their characters.

Certainly the nature of my calling involves pointing out shortcomings and mistakes, but I pursued my task with gleeful vengeance. I hammered everyone else's foibles while lightly dusting my own with the powder puff of understanding.

You hypocrite!

I bored an optical hole in the page, harpooned by the realization I had become precisely the type of individual Jesus despised: pompous, arrogant, self-righteous. With a rationalizing convenience I'd forgotten to ask myself one important question:

Who am I to judge?

* * * * *

Back at my desk, the words came quickly.

When I answered the phone, I wasn't surprised to hear a familiar voice. "How's the sermon, Doctor?"

"Coming along, Henry," I answered. "I found your little reminder, and the sermon's going to be just fine."

MAUNDY THURSDAY

✳

"And what does the Lord require of you but to do justice, and to love kindness, and to walk humbly with your God?"

—Micah 6:8

The Visitor Brought a Broom

"*There's someone at the door! There's* someone at the door!"

The voice drifted in through the fog of sleep. It took a while to orient myself, but after a few moments of eye-blinking bewilderment, I began to recognize the furnishings of our den. I also figured out whose voice had so rudely interrupted my sudden-death golf match with Tiger Woods.

It was my wife's. Her voice, plus some none-too-gentle nudging on the shoulder, had discontinued my dream.

"What do you want?" I slurred.

"For the three hundredth time, there's someone at the door, and I am not about to answer it at this time of night. It's probably that horrible salesman again. Tell him to get lost!"

"Oh well," I sighed. "I guess I'll just have to win the Masters some other time."

"Excuse me?"

"Never mind."

As I lurched from my easy chair, the Bible in my lap fell to the floor. I remembered I had yet to write my sermon for Sunday. I'd have to dispatch our nocturnal visitor quickly and return to my study.

While I trudged to the door, portions of Edgar Allan Poe's famous poem rambled through my mind:

> Once upon a midnight dreary, while I pondered,
>   weak and weary,
> Over many a quaint and curious volume of
>   forgotten lore—
> While I nodded, nearly napping, suddenly there
>   came a tapping,
> As of someone gently rapping, rapping at my
>   chamber door.

Funny, the things you remember from school days. Then it hit me—I hadn't heard anything. I stopped . . . waiting . . . listening for the bell to ring. Like a sleepwalking statue, I stood there, and heard . . . nothing.

The years move on, so I passed the incident off as another of my spouse's auditory malfunctions. I turned and headed for the den.

Then I heard it! Or thought I did. Stopping mid-stride, I cocked my head toward the door and strained. Ah! There it was again—a light tapping. I'd have missed it for sure if I'd been moving.

Who was it? One thing for certain; it wasn't the same salesman who'd frightened my wife half to death earlier in the day. When she opened the door to see who it was, he jammed his foot in the opening. He absolutely refused to leave until she heard his pitch. He really upset her. Too bad—one bad apple.

But this couldn't be the door-to-door guy. Or could it? Another ploy, perhaps?

Then again, it might be someone calling for the United Way, or the Heart Fund, or the Cancer Foundation, or any of the other numerous charitable organizations. It might even be a kid wanting me to pledge a dollar for every minute he could spin a basketball on his finger or some such nonsense. I'm a pretty soft touch, so I vowed to be careful.

I still hadn't moved from the middle of the hallway when the "tap . . . tap . . . tap" sounded again. I hurried to the front.

Turning the knob, and cracking the door ever so slightly, I watched attentively for an eager foot to come crashing through. No foot. I remained alert, and inched the opening wider.

"Hello."

I swung the door open all the way to find the source of the greeting. For a moment I thought I recognized the youngster. At least he looked young to me—in his mid-twenties. Although I couldn't quite place him, I assumed he was one of my son's college buddies or an acquaintance of one of my daughters.

Rather than act like an idiot by asking his name, I faked like I knew him. I'd figure it out.

"Hello!" I almost shouted.

That was it. No one said anything for a while. I waited for the presentation, but the young man refused to speak, much less to promote, advertise, or attempt to sell something to me. He just stood there.

After a while, seemed like hours, I felt rather foolish. Out of desperation, I blurted, "Would you like to come in?"

He broke into a wide grin. "Yes. Thank you."

I led him to the den. Surely, my wife's excellent memory for names and faces would bail me out. She wasn't there.

"She must have gone to bed," I stammered in frustration. "Would you like some coffee?"

"Please. Thank you."

Fumbling around in the kitchen, I wracked my brain trying to place my visitor. Nothing came. He hadn't played on any of the youth sports teams I coached, nor had he participated in any of the church's scouting activities. He must be connected with my children. I would get it out of him.

With renewed confidence I returned to the den to find him sitting on the couch, looking around the room. He looked different from when I had invited him in, but I couldn't figure out exactly what it was.

I took a seat, and he turned to face me. "Read much?" he asked.

A strange question, but I was so grateful for any opportunity to avoid the subject of his identity, I plunged headlong into a discourse on my reading habits.

"Oh, yes! I enjoy reading immensely. Usually keep three or four books going at once. Mostly light stuff—mysteries, biographies, sports, but occasionally one of the classics—Faulkner, Hemingway, Dostoyevsky. And, I always work on something technical, you know, something that applies directly to my work. I make an effort . . . "

"I mean in that," he interrupted. His long, slender finger jutted out in a somewhat accusing fashion in the direction of my Bible, which was still lying on the floor where I had dropped it.

Uh-oh, I thought. This guy's some sort of a Holy Roller. He's out witnessing. I bet that's why I recognize him. I probably put him off the other day, and now he's back for his two cents worth.

Neighborhood visitation and witness suit me just fine, but I didn't have time to be evangelized right then, So, I started looking for ways to get rid of my guest—politely. Meanwhile, there was nothing else to do but talk.

"Yes," I replied to his question, "I read the Bible every day. You might say it's my manual of operations. I'm a preacher, and that volume is how I make my living."

The minute I said it, I realized my mistake, but it was too late.

"Is that all it means to you, my friend?" he asked.

"No, no, of course not! It's the foundation of my faith. It's everything I believe. I was just being flippant."

Without any reaction to my verbal anemia, he pointed again, this time to the window.

"Look outside and tell me what you see."

Having settled comfortably in my chair, I was not about to comply with such a ridiculous request. I tried to remain composed.

"That's our backyard," I replied. "I'll describe it for you if you like, but at present, there's nothing to see. It's too dark and our yard's not lighted."

"Look anyway, please."

More in a state of confusion than obedience, I went to the window, drew back the curtain, and peered out into what should have been the darkness.

What I saw was not the shadowy gloom of my backyard, but a narrow city street. I recognized it as one of the more notorious areas downtown. Refuse filled the gutters on both sides of the avenue. A derelict stumbled, then fell on his face on the sidewalk. To my dismay, no one offered to help him. Instead, merchants continued to converse with customers, and ragged children played stickball in the road.

I wheeled around to my guest. Again, I noticed he looked a little different, but I still couldn't place it.

"What does this mean?" I asked, trying to stay calm. "Where is my backyard?"

My guest sipped his coffee and looked right through me. "Three weeks ago, weren't you asked to serve on a committee to help redevelop that area?"

"Why, yes," I stammered, "But I told the mayor I was too busy. It's true! There are things I need to take care of. My parishioners need me. So does my family. I work hard. I can't serve on every committee."

"Look again," he said.

I admit curiosity got the best of me, and I looked out to see a church, or rather, what was left of one. The roof had caved in, and what little remained was merely a heap of smoldering rubble.

Turning back to my guest, I explained, "That's the Mt. Bethel Holiness Church. They had a fire two weeks ago, and the . . . "

He broke in, "And the membership asked to use your facilities."

"Yes," I replied. "They were more than welcome to worship with us, but they have meetings four, five times a week. They'd have been in our building an awful lot, and we have to make sure our facilities are available for our people when they want to use them—if they want to use them. I really wasn't too pumped up about sharing my study. Some of my books are pretty valuable. Anyway, we might have worked something out, but it was easier to send them to someone else who has more room and a bigger staff."

He had changed again. Now I could tell what it was. If he was twenty-five when he entered, he was now easily sixty-five. He was grayer, thinner, weaker looking . . . almost frail. Still, he pointed to the window.

I turned to see the exercise yard at the State Penitentiary, fifteen miles east. Immediately, I remembered the call from the warden. "Preacher, how 'bout coming out here for a short while on Wednesday evenings and leading some recreation and a short devotional for the fellas?"

I'm a regular visitor out there. I go to see the inmates four or five times a year, and I really wanted to help. But Wednesdays are the night my wife and I get together with our best friends. It's sort of a tradition. I turned to explain.

The pitiful mass of flesh on the couch looked more dead than alive. I couldn't tell how old he was. I tried to speak, but nothing came out. His voice was still strong, though, and it slashed like a razor.

"You're not the only one who wouldn't go, or couldn't help, or wasn't able to find the time. For some it's card night, others have movie night, parties, lessons, meetings, weekends at the lake, quick trips for 'R and R,' late nights on the town. Some were just too tired. The list never ends. Male, female, young, old, it doesn't matter. Everyone has excuses. Look again."

"I can't."

His bony finger pointed to the window like that of one of Scrooge's uninvited guests. Fighting back the tears, I turned to the window.

Way off in the distance, a solitary cross stood on a hill. Despite the distance, the cross seemed large. The longer I gazed at it, the bigger it became, until finally, it completely filled the view. From behind, I heard the faint voice of my guest, *"Just as you did not do it to one of the least of these, you did not do it to me."*

Then it hit me. Even as I knew who he was, I realized why I had not been able to find my wife. The visit had taken place not in the den of our home, but in the sitting room of my heart. I whirled around, but he was not there.

Overcome simultaneously with joy and fear, exuberance and shame, I slumped in my chair, my face in my hands.

"Come back, please come back. I'll . . . I'll do better. I'll start over. I'll re-do all those things I did sloppily. We'll start new programs . . . rework . . . rebuild. I promise! Please, come back!"

"Wake up! Wake up!" My wife was shaking me, calling me. I awoke with a start, sweat pouring from my face.

"You've been in that chair all night," she scolded. "You'll be stiff as a board. Are you all right? You were having a nightmare."

"Yeh. Yes. Okay. I'm, uh, fine," all said more in an effort to convince myself than her. "Could, uh, I have some coffee please?"

Although slightly more disheveled, and a good deal more disturbed than when I had sat down the previous evening, I was in the same chair, in the same room, with my Bible in my lap opened to the same place. I stared down at the page and read the passage I had selected the night before as my Sunday text:

> Behold, I stand at the door and knock;
> if anyone hears my voice and opens the
> door, I will come in to him and eat with
> him and he with me.

I remembered the admonition from Revelation spoken to the church at Laodicea—the lukewarm church—a collection of Christians who existed in a state of suspended animation, neither hot nor cold, devoid of enthusiasm. They merely went through the motions, acting their parts rather than living them.

My visitor had tried to show me I was the same way. He came unobtrusively, waiting for my invitation before he entered. And though he never raised his voice, he had not hesitated in the direct fashion by which he pointed out the dust gathering on my commitment.

Now I knew what to say on Sunday. I admitted Christ when he knocked, but admission is not enough. I accepted him as my Savior, but words alone will not suffice.

No, I wasn't about to abandon all my leisure activities, put on a burlap sack, and take up the life of a hermit. But the time had more than arrived for me and those in my charge to put our priorities in order, to give a little more time, a little more effort, a little more self. Christ had knocked. And he awaited an answer.

Stretching to unkink some of the knots in my back, I walked over to the piano and thumbed through the hymnal until I found the tune running through my head. This would work at the closing:

> Lord, speak to me that I may speak
>   In living echoes of Thy tone;
> As Thou hast sought, so let me seek
>   Thy erring children lost and lone.
> O lead me, Lord, that I may lead
>   The wandering and the wavering feet;

O feed me, Lord, that I may feed
　　Thy hungry ones with manna sweet.

My eyes skipped to the last stanza, now particularly significant:

O use me, Lord, use even me.
　　Just as Thou wilt and when and where;
Until Thy blessed face I see,
　　Thy rest, Thy joy, Thy glory share.

GOOD FRIDAY

*

"For God so loved the world that he gave ..."

—John 3:16

Six Days in the Life
of a Tentmaker

never intended to join the crowd. When I started to my shop that Sunday, everything seemed normal. Just another first day of just another week. But then Ezra grabbed my arm.

"Joshua! Joshua! Are you deaf? I've been chasing you since you passed my house. Where are you going?"

"Where do you think, my old friend? Where have I gone every Sunday since you've known me? To work. Someone has to finish the tents if the Passover guests are going to have somewhere to sleep."

"But the Galilean is coming. Have you heard of him? Pretty radical stuff he throws out, but the stories! Oh, that one can fairly spin a yarn."

I knew of the Galilean—Jesus—from Nazareth. Not much of a town, but not everyone can live in the city. I'd even heard him preach once in a synagogue where I was visiting. He handled himself well enough, poised, good voice, but I felt a little uncomfortable when he read from the book of the prophet and announced, "Today this scripture has been fulfilled in your hearing." No one should say that.

As I said, I'd heard him, and the others. After a while, all those wandering minstrel soothsayers begin to sound alike. Consequently, I had very little interest in accompanying Ezra. There was work to do, a lot of it, and precious little time.

But Ezra insisted. So, to appease my dear friend, and to avoid his predictable accusation of "stick-in-the-mud," I agreed to wander along with him for a while. Besides, my employees hardly knock themselves out on Sunday even if I am there, so I had very little to lose.

By the time we arrived at the city gate there must have been two or three hundred people. Men and women of all ages pushed and shoved for a spot nearer the road. The children—everywhere, children—laughed, shouted, giggled, played, and ran. What a festival!

Someone handed me a palm branch. Then I noticed everyone had one. Who collected and distributed them I have no idea, but the road appeared surrounded by a wide, leafy ribbon of green. The crowd stood four and five deep, and still the people poured out of the city.

Everyone peered up the road toward Bethphage.

"Joshua, I haven't seen this many people in years."

"You're right, Ezra, at least not since the new governor arrived, what . . . seven years ago?"

"Yes, but the crowd was different then—frightened or something."

"I think a better word is 'angry,' Ezra. Every time we get a new prefect it reminds us we are a conquered people. It makes my blood boil just to think of it. I hate the Romans."

"Careful, Joshua. Ears, you know. Look! What's that? Here he comes!"

I couldn't see for a while—too many people. But finally I could make him out, sitting astride a donkey—a young animal, maybe a year to a year and a half old.

On the rare occasions when he looked up, the Galilean smiled in a wan sort of way. He even waved once or twice. But most of the time, he rode with his head bowed, as if lost in thought—or embarrassed.

Even when he was quite a ways off, I could hear folk yelling to him. The cheer rippled its ways toward us.

> *Hosanna to the Son of David! Blessed is*
> *he who comes in the name of the Lord.*
> *Save us, Master. Hosanna! Hosanna!*

People went crazy waving palms, like this was a conquering general or a visiting dignitary. A few folk began throwing their cloaks and palms on the road.

> *Make smooth the King's path. Hosanna*
> *in the highest.*

I'd been leaning on my palm branch like a staff. I guess I got caught up in the excitement because the next thing I knew, I was waving it for all I was worth. As the noise grew, I even began to shout:

> *Jesus . . . Jesus . . . save me, too.*
> *Hosanna, Son of David! Blessed be*
> *your name!*

When I got home, late, hoarse, and cold, I realized I didn't have my cloak. My wife chewed me out when I told her I'd thrown it onto the entry road into the city to help smooth the traveler's path.

"That was stupid!"

"I know," I said as contritely as possible. "But, at the time, it seemed like the thing to do."

* * * * *

Friday found me in the crowd, too. The size of the gathering surprised me. Pretty early for such a large number to assemble.

This crowd differed dramatically from Sunday's; not a crowd at all. More like a mob. More than a few had been drinking, some to the point of drunkenness. Later, I heard whispers that the Pharisees were responsible; that they'd passed out free wine to the rabble and encouraged everyone to drink his fill. Surely that wasn't accurate.

The Lord must have blushed that day. Sons and daughters of Israel employing filthy language, gutter talk like the Romans. A murderous mood; animals frenzied by the smell of blood.

The Galilean was there again. I'd been working hard all week. Demand for tents increased daily, so I hadn't seen his doleful countenance, but I'd heard about him. So had everyone else in Jerusalem.

Early on, he'd played the role of the hero. Monday and Tuesday he basked in the reflected glory of the big parade. Every time he sat down to rest, dozens gathered to hang on his slightest and most insignificant word. Oh, a few grumbled when he ran the bird merchants and money changers out of the Temple, but I noticed the ones who complained the most had some vested interest, so I wrote off their gripes to greed.

By Wednesday, however, things started to change. Maybe the novelty wore off. Maybe people started to figure out the extent of the trouble in which the Galilean could entangle them. Whatever the reason, the rumors began to circulate.

Some said he cursed the Temple. Others vowed he promised to destroy it. Some reported the Galilean was raising an army to lay siege to Jerusalem. Ezra heard from his wife's sister-in-law (usually a very reliable source) that the man from Nazareth told people to quit paying their taxes.

Lunacy! A civil uprising would bring the Roman war eagle screaming out of the sky. The young man might get away with a little criticism of the Pharisees, but he'd better leave the Romans alone.

Some of the things I heard seemed completely out of character from the quiet, retiring man I'd seen slumped on a donkey earlier in the week— that he'd declared himself "King." It didn't sound right, but so many said it was true.

He finally went too far. The reports got so tangled I cannot claim to know the exact order, but the content is essentially correct.

Thursday evening, the Pharisees arrested him. The charge? First, I heard blasphemy: he claimed to be The Anointed One! Then, someone said he was accused of treason: that he defied the authority of Pilate and Caesar and promised to overthrow the government.

The Temple Guard found him in Gethsemane. They took him away, but not before one of the Galilean's ruffians assaulted Malchus, the High Priest's servant. And I thought the preacher's main message dealt with peace.

The stories flew: a secret trial before the Sanhedrin . . .

witnesses who could not agree . . .

the Galilean had been tortured into a confession . . .

one report had Caiaphas asking illegal, leading questions, and Nicodemus, one of the most respected of all Pharisees, actually speaking in behalf of the accused.

Wild, unsubstantiated tales. But one fact stared us in the face: the man, the Galilean, standing on the portico of Pilate's palace. What a change. Sunday, he had looked healthy, strong, robust. Now, he appeared pitiful—and old.

That he'd been beaten could not be concealed. The bruises on his arms and face bore witness to the cudgeling. Every so often, the Galilean staggered, but somehow he kept his feet.

Beside him stood another: Barabbas—renegade, highwayman, subversive. Barabbas threw his manacled arms into the air to acknowledge the astonishing accolades of the crowd. Whenever Pilate turned his head, Barabbas spat on the ground, sneered contemptuously, or made obscene gestures. His belligerence lathered the crowd, and even before Pilate asked for a vote, the mob growled:

Barabbas, Barabbas! Give us Barabbas!

Pilate raised his hand, grinding the crowd to a begrudging silence:

*And what should I do with the other—
the one from Galilee?*

Someone yelled, "Let him go!" but he was knocked to the ground. Another shouted, "He can rot in prison." Scattered applause. Still another, "Flog him again!" The cauldron of a crowd bubbled with grim suggestions, each more gruesome than its predecessor.

Then, a blood-chilling scream pronounced the most hideous of words:

Crucify him!

For a moment, it appeared the idea would die. But suddenly, as a wave builds from nothing to a great crest, the chant began at the back, rushing forward in an ever-increasing crescendo, and crashing against the stones of the portico:

Crucify! Crucify! Crucify!

I don't really know why I ever said that word. Had I not mentioned it, crucifixion might never have surfaced. It was I who first called, "Crucify!" and, when the crowd took up the note, I led the foot-stomping and the fist-waving.

I don't know why. It just seemed like the thing to do.

* * * * *

I was also in the crowd late in the afternoon. We followed him all the way up to the Place of the Skull, mocking his every fall, cheering every lash, applauding every child whose stone found its mark. And we booed when the African took his place under the cross.

The Romans hoisted the scaffold against the morning sky and we shouted our approval. The day aged steadily. The Galilean's skin began to dry, crack, and bleed. The jeering droned on, and I buzzed along with the others:

> *Why don't you save yourself, King of the Jews? Call Elijah for help. Walk down off the cross and I will follow you.*

We had a great time: laughing, joking, watching the soldiers gamble for his clothes. Imagine, I spent an entire afternoon ridiculing a dying man. Not something of which I am proud, but, at the time, it seemed like the thing to do.

* * * * *

They took him down at three o'clock. Already dead. Most don't die so quickly on the cross, but the Galilean had been badly abused before they strung him up, I wasn't surprised.

As soon as the soldiers removed him, a few of his friends surrounded the corpse, washing his wounds, wrapping the body. One woman just held his head in her lap and stroked his hair.

I swaggered over. One parting shot. An end to this fiasco by the originator of the idea of grim death. Just as I opened my mouth to snarl, one of his friends draped a cloak over the lifeless body.

Suddenly, I remembered another cloak—thrown on the road—tossed to smooth the path of a traveler—this man—the man for whom I had cheered—the rider to whom I had waved and shouted—the Galilean whom I helped execute.

I stood for a long time, long after Ezra and my other friends sniggered their way down the slope, long after the little funeral procession staggered off. I stood there and stared at the cross that had been my suggestion.

✳ ✳ ✳ ✳ ✳

I understand the Sunday of the Palms has become a significant celebration for those who still follow the Galilean. It makes me wonder . . .

On that day, when you shout:

> *Hosanna, blessed is he who comes in the name of the Lord!*

When you sing praises in honor of the Galilean, do you do it because you love him—or because it seems like the thing to do?

SATURDAY

✳

"It is I, Jesus, who sent my angel to you . . ."

—Revelation 22:16

Which Jesus?

y life began quietly enough, good family, good training. Mother made sure I learned my manners. Father made sure I used them.

I was pretty much a model child: young Barabbas, son of a respected and learned rabbi, little Jesus Barabbas. You're surprised by my first name? Shouldn't be. Rather common, actually. And, for a while, a common life.

As far as I can remember, every day seemed the same . . .

up at dawn . . . morning prayers . . .

breakfast with the family . . . off to classes . . .

home in the afternoon . . .

various chores, then a brief respite for play . . .

assignments . . . dinner . . . evening prayers . . .

bedtime.

Day after day, every day. Except for the Sabbath. Oh, the Sabbath—my favorite day. No work. No play, either. Mostly just prayers and Temple, Temple and prayers. Only natural, I guess, what with a rabbi as a father.

My sister hated it. I'm not sure she goes to Temple anymore except, of course, at Passover. But not me. I loved it: the ritual, the solemnity, the cantor with his long, breathless lines of melody, the singing of songs, everything. But best of all, I loved the stories.

Every Sabbath afternoon, Father sat with me (outside—weather permitting), and after we recited some psalms, he would recount for me the great tales of our heritage . . .

the treachery of Adam's murderous son . . .

the fidelity of Noah and Abraham . . .

the strength and the foolishness of Samson . . .

the gallant David slaying the giant, Goliath . . .

and, best of all, the heroics of the Maccabees, mighty and unconquerable warriors.

Hour upon hour I soaked in the same, wonderful narratives until I knew them by heart. Father's eyes gleamed as he recalled the ancient days when our beloved nation battled the enemies of Jehovah and proved victorious. And every so often he would whisper his secret hope that one day Israel would again stand as a colossus among nations—free and confident.

I am not exactly sure when or how, but somewhere along the line, I adopted my father's dream as my mission.

❋ ❋ ❋ ❋ ❋

One passionate moment forever changed my life. I was already a man, in my fourteenth year, and aiming, I guess, for a career as a rabbi. Father often wondered aloud if the great teachers at the Jerusalem Seminary would tolerate my patriotic outbursts, but he also remembered when he was young and full of idealistic fight.

It happened on the type of day that makes you feel lucky to be alive and absolutely convinces you of the presence of God: warm but not hot, a pleasant sun, the shield of a gentle breeze, the birds chirping, a day of promise.

I was working in the garden, turning soil for my mother, when I heard a commotion around the side of the house. Naturally curious, I scurried to investigate.

A Roman cavalry officer had dismounted and was flailing away at an old man with his riding crop. Outrage flushed the officer's cheeks. His helmet lay in the middle of the road where he'd apparently thrown it, and he swung his whip with such violence, I feared for the old man's life.

"Jewish dog," the officer snarled. "I'll teach you to startle my horse. If you have injured Xerxes, I will kill you, but for now, you will learn a lesson in respect."

There, in front of me, a living, breathing parable of my country, outmatched and cowering before a cruel and arrogant foreigner. The Holy Nation. God's People, the Select of Almighty Jehovah, enslaved by a race of thugs!

Suddenly, the beating stopped. The old man picked himself up and looked at the prone figure of the cavalry officer. He stared in horror, switching his gaze from the Roman's crushed skull to the bloody shovel I still clutched in my white knuckles.

"Run, boy," he said. And he disappeared.

The legend swelled with time: Jesus Barabbas—killer of Romans. Only killed the one, actually, but, to tell the truth, I never did much to dispel the growing tales of glory.

What a life, living on the run, stealing from wealthy Romans to buy our food, finding assistance from only-too-happy-to-help countrymen and women.

I threw in my lot with the Zealots, only one of many resistance groups but the best by far. And very quickly I moved up in the ranks. We made jackals of the Imperial Roman visitors. They could not catch a cold, much less Jesus Barabbas. The stories of our exploits expanded so rapidly, I cannot now discern between what I really remember and what I've heard so often I only think I remember.

Don't for a moment think I did anything for my own glory. Our mission never wavered: expel the Roman eagle and restore the Lion of Judah. The plan might have worked, too. Our ranks increased with every passing day. We managed to plant Zealots and other patriots in almost every meaningful position and organization. But the occupational administration changed.

He was a sly one, the new governor, this Pilate. "Pompous" we called him—"Pompous Pilate." But though I made fun of him to my colleagues, in truth, he scared me. He possessed a whole new approach. Ruthless and clever, he refused to accept the incompetence that his predecessor seemed to perpetuate.

As if overnight, we began to lose ground— reports of trials, arrests, executions. They strung our companions on crosses, public crucifixions on the Killing Hill, hoping we would stage a rescue attempt. I knew better, but the reports of my brave comrades' struggles made sleep elusive.

One day we seemed poised to reclaim the glory of Solomon. The next, we huddled wherever we could find shelter, flinching at every noise and knock. We still raided a little, had to eat something, but the flair and daring rapidly evaporated. Even I recognized the difference between bravery and foolishness.

How they caught me I cannot prove, but I'm absolutely convinced someone sold me out. Believing one of my friends betrayed me hurts, but only a handful knew my hideout: Jacob, Joshua, Enoch, Simeon, and the Iscariot. Later, I heard rumors that one of our company had flashed around a lot of money, interestingly enough the standard Roman bounty: thirty pieces of silver. But the issue hardly matters anymore.

✳ ✳ ✳ ✳ ✳

I'd only been in custody a few days when the Governor sent for me; long enough to endure a few good thumpings at the hands of those I'd previously humiliated and frustrated, but no permanent damage. Anyway, one minute I'm in a stinking cell, the next thing I know, I'm outside, a little early in the morning for my particular tastes, but anything to get away from the mold and the rats.

So there I stood, on the expansive portico of the governor's residence, and with the Imperial Majesty himself. He didn't speak to me, of course, but he took time to size me up. I could tell he wondered how anyone as pitiful looking as I appeared at that moment had managed to cause him so much grief. His face twitched with a smile of triumph, and them he turned away.

I recognized what was happening: Passover Eve, the customary release of a prisoner. Pilate wanted to see if I proved satisfactory to the inhabitants of Jerusalem. Why they'd go to so much trouble to catch me, only to let me go, I could not fathom then, but in retrospect I understand my little band and I were not the force we imagined.

The Galilean's presence puzzled me. Yes, I knew him, at least who he was. I made it my business to know everyone in the public eye. We'd thought of using him at one time, but the Iscariot assured us of the folly of the plan. This one, it seemed, taught peace and love. What a fool! Rome understands only power.

At first, I assumed both of us would enjoy release, and for a moment a sort of unspoken

alliance formed. Ironic, I thought, both of us pris-
oners, both of us scheduled for release, oh yes,
and both of us with the same name. I looked over
at this other Jesus and nodded. Without ever
acknowledging my glance, he lowered his head.

As soon as Pilate began to address the crowd,
however, any thought of friendship with the
Galilean disappeared. The Governor made it
abundantly clear only one of us would see the sun
rise again.

"Citizens of Jerusalem," he began, "as is the
Imperial custom, Rome honors your holiest of cel-
ebrations with a gift: the release of a prisoner. You
know both these men. They seem important to
you. So, today you have a choice. Citizens of
Jerusalem, it's up to you. Whom do you wish for
me to release? Which Jesus?"

You know what happened. They took the
Galilean away and cut me loose. And I know what
they did to him. In fact, I started to go and pay my
respects but my friends wouldn't let me. They
were right. How long the pardon would last, who
could say? No use gaining freedom only to get
arrested three hours later at the Killing Hill.

❋ ❋ ❋ ❋ ❋

Well, that's my story, at least the part with
which you have concern. But before I leave, I
want to tell you one thing more, something I've
never told anyone.

I've heard all your stories about that day on the
portico. I am familiar with the written accounts,

how they relate that once we stood together the Galilean never spoke, that he bore the injustice and agony on the moment without a word. Well, that's not exactly accurate.

Pilate stood to my left; the Galilean to my right. Never before and never again has history seen such a meeting of opulence and despair. Pilate in his snow-white toga. The Galilean in rags.

Pilate posed his question: "Which Jesus?"

Silence hung over the courtyard like a thick fog. My friends wanted me, I am sure, but they would not yell for fear of imprisonment. They were not about to announce publicly their allegiance to a known revolutionary.

The Galilean's people must have felt the same way. No one so much as peeped. What if the whole situation constituted a setup, a way to lure our individual supporters out into the open for arrest and execution?

Again, the question, Pilate asking it in a different way to remove confusion: "Which do you want: Jesus Barabbas or Jesus called 'Christ'?"

Still, the crowd stood mute.

Pilate could scarcely hold rein over his anger and impatience: "I ask you again. Which Jesus?"

Then, the Galilean spoke, not loudly, but in a voice that neither wavered nor trembled. He absolutely knew what he was saying.

"Barabbas," he said. "Give them Barabbas."

And the crowd took up his recommendation.

✳ ✳ ✳ ✳ ✳

Many years have come and gone since I stood on display with the Galilean, but I will never forget what he did.

Not too long ago, I heard a man named Paul speak. I don't pretend to understand everything he described, but one thing sticks in my mind. In his address, Paul talked about the Galilean. "Jesus," he said, "Jesus of Nazareth, called the Christ, died for you."

As I freely admitted, I don't exactly know what that means to anyone else. But I fully realize that once, on a day of fear and choice, the Galilean surely died for me.

EASTER DAY

✳

*"The grace of the Lord Jesus be with all the saints.
Amen."*

—Revelation 22:21

The Resurrection Rain

Generally, we have two assumptions about Easter, both of which may be mistaken. First, we imagine the morning of the resurrection was a beautiful, bright, sunny day. Second, we assume the disciples took one look at the tomb and immediately understood exactly what had happened. This story turns these assumptions around.

he rain began *Friday* . . . *torrents* . . . sheets of water . . . horrifying buckets of tears as heaven wept for the "brightest and best of the morning's sons." The Sabbath offered no reprieve—only a solid, wet-grey blaze—a soaking scourge—slapping its rhythmic keening on sand and stone—a lamenting and lamentable Day of Rest.

Now, the first day of the week, and still the skies draped themselves in an envelope of grief.

The heavens cried, and so did John. He sobbed and cursed and shattered dishes as his almost notoriously quiet demeanor collapsed under the weight of heartache. He stood at the window and shrieked into the soggy abyss:

"Father? Wonderful! He said to call you 'Abba'—'Daddy'—as if we were truly children. Where were you in his hour of need? What did you do? Nothing! You just turned your back and pulled the curtain closed. Even now, your Creation does your mourning for you. Father God? I think not!"

Somewhere out there, the sun struggled to mount its chariot, but the usually blazing monarch of the morning could do little other than lighten the firmament's demeanor from black to the color of charcoal ash. And still the rain came, whispering gruesome reminders to John of . . .

a stumbling walk . . .

the shouts . . .

the reading of the charges . . .

the proclamation of death . . .

and that obscene cross.

John squinted at the early morning drip and shook his head. "Water, always water," he mumbled.

It made little sense. But as he thought back, from the very beginning, even in this unforgiving and arid land, his friend Jesus—the Master— had been surrounded by water.

✳ ✳ ✳ ✳ ✳

"Behold the Lamb of God who takes away the sins of the world!"

"When the Baptist shouted like that, we couldn't believe it." Andrew's face beamed as he recalled the past for John. "After all, we'd waited for so long—heard prophecies every day about the coming of the Anointed One, and suddenly, there he was."

The longer Andrew spoke, the more excited his voice grew. "The Master stepped into the river and spoke to the Baptist for a while. They seemed to disagree momentarily. Then, the Master took the Baptist's hand and placed it atop his own head. The Baptist nodded and performed the ritual of baptism.

"As soon as Jesus came out of the water, the Baptist had a vision. He screamed, more in delight than in horror, pointed to the Master, and recited the prophet's dream:

Here is my servant, whom I uphold,
   my chosen, in whom my soul delights;
I have put my spirit upon him;
   he will bring forth justice to the nations.
He will not cry or lift up his voice,
   or make it heard in the street; . . .
He will not grow faint or be crushed
   until he has established justice in the earth;
and the coastlands wait for his teaching.

"John," Andrew continued, "We all stared at him—this almost anonymous Galilean—lean, wiry, covered with the contents of the Jordan, and before our very eyes, he changed.

"The water beaded up on him like diamonds. His wet hair looked like a halo of pearls. As drenched as he was, he looked like a king!"

Yes, John thought. He always looked like a king. John folded his hands beneath his chin and watched the rain.

✳ ✳ ✳ ✳ ✳

When Nathanael related the event, fire flashed in his eyes and his voice trembled slightly.

"No one had ever seen a more festive day in Cana. My little home town seldom hosts extravagant social events, so the wedding surpassed anything we'd ever experienced. After all, the leading citizen's only daughter was getting married, so it was very special.

"We had all walked up the nine miles from Nazareth the prior afternoon. Peter, Andrew, and I accompanied the Master. I spent most of the morning showing off my small village. Not really much to see, but they at least feigned interest, especially in the family orchard. Everyone except Peter, as you might suspect—weren't any boats to hold his rather one-sided attention. Anyway, it meant a lot to me to introduce the Master and my new friends to all my loved ones.

"The wine flowed freely at the wedding celebration, and I wasn't the only one to overeat. Pastries and fruits, goat cheese and sweet breads—all piled so high you could scarcely see over them—disappeared at lightning speed. The servants ran so fast and worked so hard to replenish everything, I'm surprised their legs didn't fall off.

"The woman who spoke to the Master startled me with her beauty. 'Son,' she said, 'Son, we have a problem. Can I speak with you?'

"The two of them huddled for a moment and then the Master returned with a wry grin on his face.

"'It seems our esteemed host faces a little predicament,' he began. 'He either under-prepared or over-invited. Whatever the reason, the wine supply is threatened with extinction. I imagine we should assist him.'"

Nathanael grinned broadly and puffed out his chest a little. "I helped get everything together— six stone jars which we filled to their brims with water. When the Master told us to taste the contents of the first vessel, we all sort of looked at each other. I mean, we'd just finished topping them off from the well.

"I went first, skimming the ladle across the top until it overflowed. What I poured down my throat amazed me—the richest, heartiest wine I've ever known.

"We scurried over to the chief butler, encouraging him to serve what he assumed he'd overlooked. And when he restocked the party's flagging liquid reserves, all the guests marveled at this newly proffered nectar.

"Every time one of the revelers sipped the results of his work, the Master clapped his hands in delight. Never before, and never since, have I seen him as he was that day—full of joy—a child at play."

John shook his head at the recollection: a man of laughter faced with a life of pain. He stretched a kink out of his lower back and stared back at the rain.

✻ ✻ ✻ ✻ ✻

Although John had witnessed the episode, he preferred to hear Peter recount it. After all, reciting the incident was the only thing the boisterous old sea dog did quietly. Peter particularly enjoyed telling the tale to children.

"The squall hit us without warning," Peter said. "None of us expected it—no signs—no indication of any kind. Andrew never even smelled it, and nothing gets past that nose of his."

The youngsters usually giggled because Andrew always feigned anger at his brother's comment, and covered his rather prominent beak with his hands, as if embarrassed.

Peter continued, "The heavens opened and the tempest hit like it was aimed right at us. Fifteen-foot swells pitched and battered our little boat. I've ridden out many a storm, but at that moment, I had never been so sure I was about to sink.

"We began to bail because we were taking on water. We cleared the boat as fast as we could, but the end was not far off—I could tell.

"Suddenly, I looked up—I don't know why, I had plenty to do—and there . . . there I saw the Master. He looked like a ghost—an apparition. Thomas even screamed and began to pray. The wind howled and the waves lashed at the Master, and still he drew closer and closer to us as if walking on the water.

"I stood up and called out, 'Lord, if it is you, tell me to come to you over the sea!' And he said, 'Come.' What I tell you is absolutely true—I promise. If you don't believe me, ask one of the others. They all saw it.

"I took five full steps on the water toward him. Just as I am standing here, I walked upon the sea.

"You ask what happened next? Hold on—patience! I'll tell you. I kept moving toward the Master, confidence growing with every stride, and then a huge swell crested and hit me. I panicked, I guess, and I turned back to look at the boat. I took my eyes off the Master for a moment, but the next thing I knew, the waters were crawling past my chest.

"I've never yelled so loudly in all my life, 'Lord, save me!' Terror began to choke me. I knew I would drown.

"But the Master reached down, hauled me into the boat, and the winds died. Then, he looked at me, and said, 'Peter, what happened? You were doing so well!'

"You shake your head, little one? I do not blame you. Had I not been there . . . if I had not been the one standing over the storm with him, I would never have believed it possible. But that one—that one over there is special.

"He may look small, my young friends, and right now the dust of the road stains his face and mats his hair, but within the breast of that man called Jesus beats a heart greater than any lion's and rests a power . . . " (and here, Peter always whispered)—"a power greater even than Caesar's."

"Power?" John bolted from his seat and flung an unlit lamp against the wall. "Where is your power now?"

In an effort to control his rage, he leaned against the wall. And still the rain came.

* * * * *

The six hours on Golgotha had limped along; each minute an agonizing gasp for breath. Six hours of humiliation. Six hours of ridicule. Six hours of torment. Then, with a shout, the torture ended, at least for the Master. His bleeding forehead dropped and lolled to the left, his biceps collapsed, his heaving chest deflated.

One of the sentries prodded him with the butt end of a spear. Then, as if to signal—or perhaps to ensure—the end, the soldier flipped the weapon over and, with the razor-sharp blade, opened a long, red fissure in the Master's side.

Water gushed from the wound. This time, not the fluid of the Jordan's coronation . . .

or Cana's celebration . . .

or the surrender of the Galilean Sea.

This was a flood of terror: the water of death.

John slumped back into his chair, and closed his eyes, trying desperately to clear the grisly scene from his mind.

* * * * *

"John?" A voice strained through his reverie and bounced him back into the painful present. He turned. Magdalene stood in the door, water dripping from her face, hair, and clothing. "John, something's wrong."

He wasn't exactly sure what she'd said. He understood the words; they just didn't make sense. Before he knew it, John was out the door, and jogging, without benefit of cloak or hat, after the figure in front of him. Peter, never one to allow the facts to interfere with his perception, had darted from the room the moment Mary opened her mouth.

At first, John trotted along. He felt no sense of urgency. But, the longer he ran, the more palpable his anger became. "They have taken the Lord out of the tomb and we do not know where they have laid him." That's what she had said.

"They have taken the Lord." The horror and humiliation of Friday welled up within him: the butchery . . . the brutality . . . the leering, sneering faces of a crowd completely unacquainted with any details of the Master's life except the lies they'd swallowed, yet thoroughly convinced of their own individual and collective righteousness. Death by strangulation on a Roman cross . . . a mutilated body . . . a borrowed grave. Now, the final insult: "They have taken the Lord."

John howled into the morning splatter, "Will you not leave him alone?" His feet slammed the ground, punishing the sod because those deserving retaliation stood out of reach. He flew past Peter whose initial impulsiveness rapidly conceded to his advancing years.

"They have taken the Lord!" John ran in fury and in fear, raced through the garden gate, hurled himself against the side of the sepulchre he'd seen only once but knew all too well, took a step toward the door, and absolutely froze.

The large, circular stone they had rolled across the opening late Friday afternoon now lay retracted in its trough. Though the mouth of the tomb yawned and beckoned, John could not move.

Peter staggered his way to the site, cast a long, quizzical look at John, then descended the short steps into the sepulchre. Peter's voice almost squeaked. "John, come here."

The younger man took a deep breath, ducked his head, and joined the fisherman.

In the corner of the cramped vault, John saw yards of linen strips lumped in a pile—a dead man's final wardrobe—graveclothes made almost lewd by their lack of an occupant. At the edge of the slab upon which they'd laid the Master's body, the head wrap lay alone—and folded.

Neither man looked at the other. Nor did either one speak. Very slowly, they turned and walked outside. Finally, Peter broke the stillness.

"John, what does this mean? Where is the Master?"

John faced his usually brash, suddenly unsure friend. "Simon, I don't know exactly. The Master said some very strange things the other evening. Do you remember?

"He said, 'A little while, and you will not see me any longer; again a little while and you will see me.'

"I'm not really sure how what he said connects with what has happened, but I'm sure it does. Right now, not much seems very clear. I understand one thing, though: Friday didn't end it. He's not finished, either with us or with the world. Peter, the Master's not finished!"

In the east, the sun broke through the clouds. Though the rain still fell, the garden began to radiate a wonderful, muggy warmth.

Splattered with mud, drenched to the skin, the rain sliding down their cheeks and mingling with tears of unrestrained joy, Peter and John stood in the drizzle, and embraced, and laughed, and bellowed in confused excitement. They danced at the door of the tomb, all the while surrounded and soaked by the wonderful, wet presence of God.

The two old friends pivoted and raced back to the house to await something they did not altogether comprehend. But whatever was to happen, they absolutely believed it would prove to be the coming of the King.